THI[S]
BEL[ONGS] ...

| Name: Thomas | Age: 9 |

| Favourite player: Marcus Tav |

2018/2019

My Predictions...   **Actual...**

Boro's final position:

| | |

Boro's top scorer:

| | |

Championship Winners:

| | |

Championship top scorer:

| | |

FA Cup Winners:

| | |

EFL Cup Winners:

| | |

Contributors: Peter Rogers & Gordon Cox

A TWOCAN PUBLICATION

©2018. Published by twocan under licence from Middlesbrough FC.

Every effort has been made to ensure the accuracy of information within this publication but the publishers cannot be held responsible for any errors or omissions. Views expressed are those of the authors and do not necessarily represent those of the publishers or the football club. All rights reserved.

ISBN 978-1-912692-30-9

PICTURE CREDITS: Middlesbrough FC, Tom Banks, Varley Picture Agency, Action Images and Press Association.

CONTENTS

01 DIMI **KONSTANTOPOULOS**

GOALKEEPER **DOB: 29/11/1978** **COUNTRY: GREECE**

Dimi made his Boro first team debut in a 2-0 FA Cup defeat to Hull City in 2014 and was part of the record-breaking Boro rearguard who racked up nine consecutive league clean sheets in the 2015/16 season, smashing a 30-year club milestone.

03 GEORGE **FRIEND**

DEFENDER **DOB: 17/10/1987** **COUNTRY: ENGLAND**

George has become one of Boro's most popular players on and off the field since joining the club from Doncaster Rovers in July 2012. He played in his 200th league game for Boro in the 2017/18 season and made 39 appearances, scoring twice, during a campaign that ended with him just one short of 350 career appearances.

SQUAD 2018/19

04 DANIEL **AYALA**

DEFENDER **DOB: 07/11/1990** **COUNTRY: SPAIN**

Ayala found his goalscoring touch in the 2017/18 season when he scored seven in 40 appearances. That put him in a small, but elite list of Middlesbrough centre-halves who have scored as many in one season. Only Willie Maddren, Tony Mowbray and Mel Nurse have reached that mark.

06 DANNY **BATTH**

DEFENDER DOB: 21/09/1990 COUNTRY: ENGLAND

Danny joined Boro on 31 August 2018 on a season-long loan from Premier League side Wolves. The centre-back joined the Academy set-up at Molineux in 2000 and became a regular in the heart of defence for Wolves and was club captain. He was also part of the Wolves squad who earned promotion to the Premier League last season.

05 RYAN **SHOTTON**

DEFENDER DOB: 30/10/1988 COUNTRY: ENGLAND

Ryan made his Boro debut on 30 September 2017 in a 2-2 draw at home with Brentford, scored his first goal in a 2-1 win away to Sheffield Wednesday on 23 December and made 28 appearances in his first season.

07 GRANT **LEADBITTER**

MIDFIELDER DOB: 07/01/1986 COUNTRY: ENGLAND

Grant is one of Boro's most consistent players and brings a wealth of experience from spells with Ipswich Town and hometown club Sunderland. He made 34 appearances in the 2017/18 season, one that saw him play in his 200th league game for Boro, pass through the 400 career start mark and close in on 500 career appearances.

08 ADAM **CLAYTON**

MIDFIELDER   DOB: **14/01/1989**   COUNTRY: **ENGLAND**

Adam is a product of the Manchester City Academy where he signed at the age of seven. A combative midfielder, he joined Middlesbrough in August 2014. He has firmly cemented himself as a first team regular and made 36 appearances in all competitions last season.

09 BRITT **ASSOMBALONGA**

STRIKER   DOB: **06/12/1992**   COUNTRY: **DR CONGO**

Boro smashed their transfer record to sign prolific striker Britt from Nottingham Forest in summer 2017. He ended his first season with Middlesbrough as top scorer, finding the net 15 times in 47 appearances (34 starts).

SQUAD 2018/19

10 MARTIN BRAITHWAITE

STRIKER **DOB: 05/06/1991** **COUNTRY: DENMARK**

A versatile forward Martin joined Boro from French side Toulouse in July 2017. After making 21 appearances with Boro, scoring six goals, he joined Bordeaux on loan for the remainder of the season. Back in Ligue 1, he made 14 appearances and scored five goals as the French side finished sixth and qualified for Europe.

11 JORDAN **HUGILL**

STRIKER DOB: 04/06/1992 COUNTRY: ENGLAND

Middlesbrough-born Jordan signed for his boyhood club on a season-long loan from Premier League side West Ham in August 2018. A latecomer to the professional game, Jordan cut his teeth in non-league with Seaham Red Star, Consett, Whitby Town and Marske, with whom he played in the North Riding Senior Cup final in 2013.

SQUAD 2018/19

14 SAM **McQUEEN**

DEFENDER DOB: 06/02/1995 COUNTRY: ENGLAND

Sam became Boro's sixth summer signing after joining from Southampton on a season-long loan in August 2018. A former England Under-21 international, Sam made his Premier League debut for Southampton in October 2016 against Burnley, with his full Saints debut coming at the San Siro against Inter Milan in the Europa League.

17 PADDY McNAIR

MIDFIELDER **DOB: 27/04/1995** **COUNTRY: NORTHERN IRELAND**

Paddy joined Boro from north-east neighbours Sunderland in June 2018. Equally adept playing in the heart of defence and midfield, Paddy represents Northern Ireland whom he helped to reach the European Championships for the first time in their history in 2016, making two appearances at the tournament.

16 JONNY HOWSON

MIDFIELDER **DOB: 21/05/1988** **COUNTRY: ENGLAND**

Jonny signed for Boro in July 2017, arriving from Norwich City for whom he made 188 appearances scoring 24 goals. He began his career with hometown Leeds United, for whom he made 221 appearances, scoring 28 goals and was 18 when he made his full debut in a 0-0 draw with Hull in December 2006.

SQUAD 2018/19

18 ASHLEY FLETCHER

STRIKER **DOB: 02/10/1995** **COUNTRY: ENGLAND**

Ashley made his Boro debut on the opening day of the 2017/18 season in a 1-0 defeat away to Wolves. He scored his first goal for the club in a 3-0 win over Scunthorpe in the second round of the Carabao Cup at the Riverside on 22 August.

19 STEWART DOWNING

MIDFIELDER **DOB: 22/07/1984** **COUNTRY: ENGLAND**

The 2017/18 season saw several landmarks for Stewart as he passed the 350 appearance mark for Boro, over 250 of those in the league, his career smash through the 600 appearance mark and 500 league appearances also reached. In total during the campaign he made 47 appearances, scoring three goals.

20 DAEL **FRY**

DEFENDER   DOB: 30/08/1997   COUNTRY: ENGLAND

Dael has been with Boro since the age of seven. At the end of the domestic season in 2018, he was named in the England U21 squad for the Toulon Tournament where he played a central role in the Young Lions securing victory for the third successive time. He was also named in the Team of the Tournament.

22 GEORGE **SAVILLE**

MIDFIELDER   DOB: 01/06/1993   COUNTRY: NORTHERN IRELAND

An international teammate of Paddy McNair, George learned his trade in the Chelsea Academy. Loans spells with Millwall and Brentford came before a permanent move to Wolves. Two more loan spells with Bristol City and Millwall, again, came before a permanent move to The Den. George featured prominently for the Lions last season, scoring 10 goals in 45 appearances as Neil Harris' side made an unexpected challenge for a Play-Off spot after a storming second half of the season. Signed for us on loan on August 31, with a view to making the deal permanent in January.

23 DARREN **RANDOLPH**

GOALKEEPER **DOB:** 12/05/1987 **COUNTRY: IRELAND**

A full Republic of Ireland international, Darren's Boro debut came in the first game of the 2017/18 season away at Wolves. He went on to become Boro's only ever-present in the league, playing all 46 games, and made 50 appearances in total in his first season with us.

24 ADEN **FLINT**

DEFENDER **DOB:** 11/07/1989 **COUNTRY: ENGLAND**

Aden became Boro's second summer signing after joining from Bristol City. He was a member of the Robins side who clinched promotion from League One and lifted the Football League Trophy in 2015, scoring the opening goal in the final. He was also named in the PFA League One Team of the Year that season.

SQUAD 2018/19

25 NATHAN **WOOD**

DEFENDER DOB: 31/05/2002 COUNTRY: ENGLAND

Nathan linked up with the Boro Academy at Under-13 level from his local side Stockton Town. He made history at the start of the 2018/19 season when he became the youngest ever player to play for Middlesbrough. He was aged 16 years 75 days when playing v Notts County in a Carabao Cup Round 1 tie on Tuesday 15 August 2018.

26 LEWIS **WING**

MIDFIELDER DOB: 23/05/1995 COUNTRY: ENGLAND

Lewis joined the club during the summer of 2017 after impressing with Northern League side Shildon. He made his first team debut as an 80th minute substitute for Grant Leadbitter in a 3-0 win over Scunthorpe United in a second round Carabao Cup tie at the Riverside in August.

27 HARRISON **CHAPMAN**

MIDFIELDER DOB: 05/11/1997 COUNTRY: ENGLAND

Hartlepool-born Harry joined Dael Fry in becoming a part of the first England squad to win a World Cup since 1966 when the Under-20s lifted the trophy in the summer of 2017. An unused substitute in the final, Harry featured in the group game against Guinea and was an important member of Paul Simpson's successful squad.

28 MARCUS **TAVERNIER**

MIDFIELDER DOB: 22/03/1999 COUNTRY: ENGLAND

Marcus joined Boro at Under-14 level and has progressed through the ranks, signing his first professional contract as a 17-year-old in October 2016. He made his first team debut starting in the side that went on to beat Scunthorpe United 3-0 in a second round Carabao Cup tie at the Riverside on 22 August 2017.

SQUAD 2018/19

31 ANDY **LONERGAN**

GOALKEEPER DOB: 19/10/1983 COUNTRY: **ENGLAND**

Andy was Boro's third arrival in August 2018. He has clocked up almost 400 appearances over a career spanning 18 years. He was understudy to Boro's current goalkeeping coach Jonathan Gould while at Deepdale and brings a wealth of experience between the sticks.

39 RUDY **GESTEDE**

STRIKER DOB: 10/10/1988 COUNTRY: **FRANCE**

Rudy signed with Boro from Aston Villa in January 2017. His 2017/18 season was decimated through two nasty injuries - in a thigh muscle and a broken ankle - and it said much for the character of the player that he still battled his way to 22 appearances and four goals.

37 MO **BESIC**

MIDFIELDER DOB: 10/09/1992
COUNTRY: BOSNIA & HERZEGOVINA

A combative midfielder, Muhamed 'Mo' Besic returned to Boro for a second loan stint in August 2018 for the 2018/19 season. He made his first Boro debut against Cardiff City in February 2018 and went on to make 17 appearances in 2017/18, scoring once against Derby County.

PRACTICE MAKES PERFECT

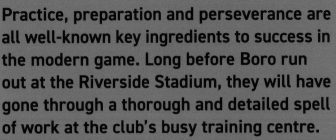

Practice, preparation and perseverance are all well-known key ingredients to success in the modern game. Long before Boro run out at the Riverside Stadium, they will have gone through a thorough and detailed spell of work at the club's busy training centre.

Boro's training ground is geared up to ensure that Tony Pulis' men are fully equipped for the Championship challenges that lie ahead. The modern-day player will not only be given the best of surfaces to practice on, but also given the very best advice and guidance in terms of their fitness, diet, rest and mental approach to performing at their maximum.

A typical day will begin with a series of physical tests, being weighed and taking part in a number of aerobic exercises, before blood levels and heart rates are measured.

Diet is vital to any player's wellbeing and performance levels, so a suitable breakfast is provided before the players head to the gymnasium to enjoy their own personal work-outs.

Prior to taking to the training pitches, players will be provided with a GPS tracking system and heart rate analysis monitors ensuring that all they do can be measured, monitored and reviewed. Then the physical conditioning begins out on the pitches. The manager and coaches will get down to working on various drills, set-piece situations and practice matches in the day's main session.

After a warm-down programme, it's off for a healthy lunch and a return to the gym for a strength, power and injury presentation session and feedback on the day's activities will be provided to the manager, coaches and players by the sports science department.

Come match day, this is where all the team's hard work and dedication through the week will make the difference.

19

16

JONNY HOWSON

BORN:

13 NOVEMBER 1960 · PAISLEY, RENFREWSHIRE

POSITION:

STRIKER

BORO DEBUT:

LEEDS UNITED 1-0 MIDDLESBROUGH
DIVISION TWO · 12 OCTOBER 1985

ALL CLUBS:

GREENOCK MORTON, AIRDRIEONIANS, QUEEN OF THE SOUTH,
ALBION ROVERS, MIDDLESBROUGH, PORT VALE, DARLINGTON

BORO APPEARANCES:

APPEARANCES	LEAGUE	FA CUP	OTHERS
381	307	19	55

BORO GOALS:

GOALS	LEAGUE	FA CUP	OTHERS
146	118	3	25

STAT ATTACK
BERNIE SLAVEN

REPUBLIC OF IRELAND INTERNATIONAL:

APPEARANCES	GOALS
7	1

INTERNATIONAL DEBUT:

28 MARCH 1990 · REPUBLIC OF IRELAND 1-0 WALES (SCORED ON DEBUT)

When Boro paid Albion Rovers £25,000 for the services of striker Bernie Slaven in the autumn of 1985, little did anyone know that the 24-year-old would go on to become one of the most popular players in the club's history.

Slaven scored 22 goals in the 1986/87 Third Division campaign as Boro won promotion at the first time of asking. His goals were once again the catalyst for promotion as Boro celebrated back-to-back promotion success in 1987/88, with Slaven netting 21 league goals to help propel the club into the First Division.

In total he scored 146 goals for the club and his fence-climbing celebrations at the Holgate End made him an iconic figure with Boro fans.

21

DANGER MEN

Watch out for these Danger Men when Boro meet their Championship rivals...

ASTON VILLA
Jack Grealish

Attacking midfielder Jack Grealish is sure to be the driving force behind Aston Villa once again in 2018/19.

The talented playmaker is a Villa fan and will be going full throttle to help Steve Bruce's side win promotion back to the Premier League. Villa were delighted to keep him at the club following a summer of speculation about the England Under-21 star's future.

BOLTON WANDERERS
Yanic Wildschut

Former Boro midfielder Yanic Wildschut joined Bolton Wanderers on a season-long loan deal from Championship rivals Norwich City in July 2018.

The talented 27-year-old, who loves to run at the opposition, enjoyed the perfect start to his Bolton career by scoring the winning goal on the opening day of the season away to West Bromwich Albion.

BIRMINGHAM CITY
Che Adams

After joining Blues from Sheffield United in August 2016, all-action midfielder Che Adams wasted little time in showing the St Andrew's faithful just what he was all about.

Adams wrote his name into Birmingham City folklore on the final day of the 2016/17 campaign, scoring the goal that preserved the club's Championship status. He is sure to be a key player for Garry Monk's men in 2018/19.

BRENTFORD
Ollie Watkins

One of the most exciting and talented footballers outside of the Premier League, Ollie Watkins has been a roaring success since joining Brentford from Exeter City in the summer of 2017.

He netted an impressive eleven goals in all competitions in his first season at Griffin Park. He loves to let fly from distance and has scored a number of spectacular goals for the Bees.

BLACKBURN ROVERS
Elliott Bennett

Experienced winger Elliott Bennett played a vital role in Rovers' promotion from League One in 2017/18.

The former Brighton and Norwich man has been a great influence on the younger players at Ewood Park and will be an important member of Tony Mowbray's team once again now they are back in the Championship.

BRISTOL CITY
Andreas Weimann

Much-travelled Austrian striker Andreas Weimann joined Bristol City ahead of the 2018/19 season, agreeing a three-year deal at Ashton Gate.

Weimann is a vastly experienced forward who knows the English game well following spells with Aston Villa, Watford, Derby County and Wolves. The Robins will be looking for Weimann to grab the goals to fire them into Play-Off contention.

DERBY COUNTY
Tom Lawrence

Wales international midfielder Tom Lawrence, looks set to play a vital role at Pride Park in 2018/19 under new Derby boss Frank Lampard.

The Rams' midfielder certainly has an eye for goal and with Lampard to guide him, Lawrence could well become one of the Championship's star turns over the coming months. He began the season in fine form with two goals in Derby's opening two games.

LEEDS UNITED
Kemar Roofe

Pacy frontman Kemar Roofe joined Leeds United in July 2016 following an impressive goalscoring spell with Oxford United.

Roofe made a great start to life under new Leeds boss Marcelo Bielsa with four goals in the opening month of the 2018/19 season, as his form earned him the Championship Player of the Month award for August 2018. The Elland Road fans will be hopeful that the lively forward can carry his impressive form into 2019.

HULL CITY
Fraizer Campbell

Vastly-experienced striker Fraizer Campbell brings an enormous amount of knowhow to the Tigers' front line.

A former England international, Campbell has spent time on the books at some of the country's biggest clubs including Manchester United and Tottenham Hotspur. Now in his second spell with Hull, he was on target against Sheffield Wednesday to ensure the Tigers' first point of the 2018/19 season.

IPSWICH TOWN
Jon Nolan

Talented midfielder Jon Nolan was an instrumental player for Shrewsbury Town in 2017/18 as the Shrews reached both the Checkatrade Trophy final and the League One Play-Off final.

In August 2018, he joined Ipswich Town and reunited with his former Shrewsbury boss Paul Hurst who took over at Portman Road three months earlier. Nolan is expected to flourish at Championship level.

MILLWALL
Steve Morison

Evergreen forward Steve Morison is currently enjoying his second spell with the Lions.

His goals helped propel the South London club to the verge of the Play-Offs last season. Over 300 games for Millwall and almost 100 goals, Morison is a vital member of Neil Harris' squad with a positive influence both on and off the pitch.

DANGER MEN

Watch out for these Danger Men when Boro meet their Championship rivals...

NORWICH CITY

Onel Hernández

Cuban-born German forward Onel Hernández provides a real spark to the Norwich City attack. He has the ability to operate down either flank or in a central striking role.

Hernández joined Norwich during the 2018 January transfer window, after agreeing a switch from German side Eintracht Braunschweig. With his speed and close control, he certainly looks like being the creative spark that can make things happen for the Canaries in attacking areas.

QUEENS PARK RANGERS

Conor Washington

Northern Ireland international striker Conor Washington made his name in the lower divisions with impressive scoring spells for Newport County and Peterborough United.

He joined Rangers in January 2016 and his all-action displays soon made him a favourite with the Loftus Road crowd. Washington will be keen to impress under former England boss Steve McClaren this season.

NOTTINGHAM FOREST

Lewis Grabban

A proven Championship goalscorer, Lewis Grabban joined Nottingham Forest in July 2018 for a fee believed to have been in the region of £6M.

His arrival at the City Ground is expected to relieve some of the pressure for goals on fellow frontman Daryl Murphy. Grabban has played for a host of clubs and appears to have the handy knack of always taking his scoring boots with him.

READING

Jon Dadi Bodvarsson

Icelandic international forward Jon Dadi Bodvarsson has become something of a cult hero with Reading fans at the Madejski Stadium after netting ten goals for the Royals last season.

He represented his country at the 2018 World Cup finals in Russia and also netted Reading's first goal of the 2018/19 campaign.

PRESTON NORTH END

Tom Barkhuizen

After beginning his career with Preston's rivals Blackpool, striker Tom Barkhuizen is a player who will be looking to make his mark for Alex Neil's side in 2018/19.

A string of loan spells with Hereford United, Fleetwood Town and Morecambe resulted in a permanent switch to Morecambe and it was his goalscoring form at the Globe Arena that alerted North End who signed him in November 2016.

ROTHERHAM UNITED

Joe Newell

Versatile midfielder Joe Newell was one of the Millers heroes as Rotherham United won promotion to the Championship via the League One Play-Offs.

With the ability to operate in a creative central midfield berth or out on the wing, Newell was almost ever-present for the Millers last season and will be a key performer for Paul Warne's men in their 2018/19 Championship campaign.

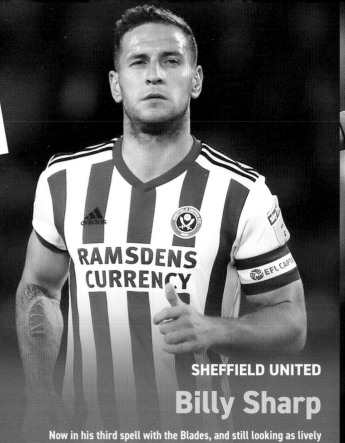

SHEFFIELD UNITED
Billy Sharp

Now in his third spell with the Blades, and still looking as lively as ever in front of goal, Billy Sharp will once again be at the forefront of manager Chris Wilder's thoughts at Bramall Lane

Sharp became the Sheffield United captain in 2016.

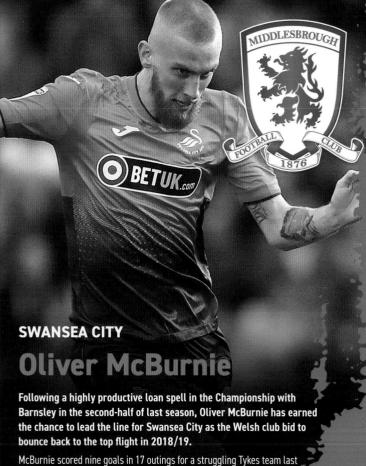

SWANSEA CITY
Oliver McBurnie

Following a highly productive loan spell in the Championship with Barnsley in the second-half of last season, Oliver McBurnie has earned the chance to lead the line for Swansea City as the Welsh club bid to bounce back to the top flight in 2018/19.

McBurnie scored nine goals in 17 outings for a struggling Tykes team last season and will now look to grab his Swansea opportunity with both hands.

SHEFFIELD WEDNESDAY
Fernando Forestieri

The jewel in Sheffield Wednesday's crown, all eyes at Hillsborough will once again be on skilful Italian Fernando Forestieri who is the man that makes the Owls tick.

The Wednesday fans will be looking for Forestieri to inspire those around him as the club searches for an improved season under Jos Luhakay.

WEST BROMWICH ALBION
Jay Rodriguez

Burnley-born England striker Jay Rodriguez began his career at his hometown club before moving on to the Premier League with Southampton and then West Bromwich Albion.

A cool customer with the ball at his feet, Rodriguez has all the skills to really shine in the Championship for an Albion side who will hope their stay in the second tier is a brief one.

STOKE CITY
Benik Afobe

Striker Benik Afobe is the man charged with scoring the goals to fire Stoke City back to the Premier League at the first time of asking.

Afobe joined the Potters on loan from Wolverhampton Wanderers in June 2018 and his physical presence and goal threat are sure to play a huge part in the Potters' 2018/19 promotion push.

WIGAN ATHLETIC
Nick Powell

Midfielder Nick Powell was nominated for the EFL League One Player of the Season award after an outstanding season in the Latics 2017/18 title-winning campaign.

A technically gifted player with the ability to score goals and create chances for others, Powell will certainly be one of the first names on Paul Cook's teamsheet as Wigan look to establish themselves at Championship level.

Magic MOMENT

FIXTURE:	Second Division Play-Off final, first leg
DATE:	Wednesday, 25 May 1988
SCORE:	Middlesbrough 2 Chelsea 0
VENUE:	Ayresome Park
ATTENDANCE:	25,531

BACK TO THE *Big Time*

Striker Trevor Senior repaid a huge chunk of his £200,000 transfer fee when he netted one of the goals in the first leg of the 1988 Play-Off final victory over Chelsea.

Having overcome Bradford City in the semi-final, Boro faced Chelsea in the two-legged final with the first leg at Ayresome Park on 25 May 1988. Senior had given the home side a 30th minute lead but when Boro legend Bernie Slaven made it 2-0 with just nine minutes remaining, Ayresome Park erupted as the Boro faithful knew the team had one foot back in the First Division.

Three days later Boro secured promotion despite losing the second leg 1-0. Slaven's goal therefore being the vital decider in taking Boro back to the big time.

BERNIE SLAVEN CELEBRATES

23

DARREN RANDOLPH

FAN TASTIC

There are five England World Cup stars hiding in the crowd... can you find them all?

#BOY'S GOT SKILLS
THE PUSKAS MOVE

Ferenc Puskas is one of the greatest footballers of all time and the creator of the famous 'V' move that you can see used in most games of football. It allows you to change direction quickly and fool your defender. The move is very simple but hard to master at speed.

TIP:
Use this move when you need to lose your defender. Pretend to strike the ball, your opponent will move to block your faked shot, allowing you to move freely in another direction.

TIP:
Always wait until your defender lunges for the ball before performing the Puskas move.

1. Start by dribbling the ball, keep it as near to your foot as possible while moving forward.

2. Move as if to kick the ball, but rather than striking it, bring your foot over the top of the ball.

TIP:
Don't perform this move too often or your opponents will learn to expect it!

3. Use the bottom of your foot to quickly drag the ball back to you.

4. Now change direction. You can finish the move with a shot at goal or by passing to a teammate.

10

MIDDLESBROUGH
FOOTBALL CLUB
1876

32Red

MARTIN
BRAITHWAITE

9

BRITT
ASSOMBALONGA

BORN:

3 SEPTEMBER 1970 · WATFORD

POSITION:

DEFENDER

BORO DEBUT:

18 AUGUST 2001 · PREMIERSHIP
MIDDLESBROUGH 0-4 ARSENAL

ALL CLUBS:

CRYSTAL PALACE, ASTON VILLA, MIDDLESBROUGH

BORO APPEARANCES:

APPEARANCES	LEAGUE	FA CUP	LEAGUE CUP	OTHERS
204	160	16	9	19

BORO GOALS:

GOALS	LEAGUE
4	4

STAT ATTACK
GARETH SOUTHGATE

ENGLAND INTERNATIONAL:

APPEARANCES	GOALS
57	2

INTERNATIONAL DEBUT:

12 DECEMBER 1995 · ENGLAND 1-1 PORTUGAL

Current England manager Gareth Southgate joined Boro from Aston Villa in the summer of 2001 for a fee of £6.5M. The switch saw him reunite with his former Villa Park defensive partner Ugo Ehiogu. The two formed a formidable partnership at the heart of the Boro defence that underpinned Steve McClaren's reign as manager.

Southgate immediately became a fans' favourite at the Riverside and was voted the club's Player of the Season during his debut campaign. The 2003/04 season saw Southgate become the first Boro captain ever to lift a national knockout trophy as he skippered the side to League Cup glory over Bolton Wanderers.

Southgate also proudly captained Boro in the UEFA Cup Final in 2006. He then served as manager from 2006 to 2009.

The season didn't start well for Adama. He wasn't in the starting line-up for the first two games and it wasn't until the third game of the campaign, a home win over Scunthorpe in the Carabao Cup, that he was seen from the start.

He turned in a terrific performance in the following game, unplayable in a 3-0 win away to Bolton and hopes were high that he was off and running.

But in the next game, away to his former club Aston Villa, he was sent-off after just four minutes. He was to be sent-off again later in the campaign, away to Sunderland, but that decision was overturned on appeal.

In between he had set the division alight, with most of his good work coming in the second half of the season when he left scorch marks on pitches around the country with his searing pace.

January saw his 22nd birthday, but rather than receive presents, his present to everyone was a greater understanding of the game, a maturity that saw him dominate matches and make the best of positions he found himself in after setting off on lightning runs - no-one could catch him.

His first goal for the club came on January 20 away to QPR. A darting run saw him scythe through the Rangers defence and drill a low shot into the bottom corner of the net with five minutes of the game remaining. It was the third in a 3-0 win for Tony Pulis' side.

Adama went on to score four more goals that season and display form that prompted a bid from Wolves that triggered a clause in his contract and he was transferred to Molineux in August for a fee of £18m.

PLAYER
OF THE SEASON

ADAMA TRAORE

GOAL
OF THE SEASON

QPR 0 MIDDLESBROUGH 3
SATURDAY 20 JANUARY 2018

There were many contenders but when the fans were asked for their thoughts there was a stand-out winner. It's not very often that a defender comes up with the Goal of the Season, but George Friend's strike against QPR in January was judged the best of the lot.

George hadn't scored in his 61 previous games - he must have been saving up for this one. It was just over two years earlier in a home win over Derby that the left-back last found the back of the net, but with 34 minutes played on a cool afternoon at Loftus Road, George edged in from the left-hand touchline, took aim and from around 25 yards from goal struck an unstoppable shot that flew into the top corner.

It was the middle of three goals Boro scored without reply that afternoon.

Daniel Ayala headed the side into a 25th minute lead after Ben Gibson had flicked on a Grant Leadbitter corner. George's goal followed nine minutes later, then with five minutes remaining Adama Traore took on the Rangers defence, skipped through it and sent a low shot into the bottom corner in front of Boro's travelling fans.

It was Adama's first Boro goal and meant as much to him as the one from the farmer's son from Devon who had a big smile on his face when he was presented with the Goal of the Season award at the end of the campaign.

George and Dani were both on the scoresheet again later in the season, in a 2-1 home win over Bristol City. Then George scored a dramatic equaliser in the 97th minute away to Millwall in the opening game of the 2018/19 season. It was a very important goal, but not as good as the one on the other side of London six and a half months earlier.

GEORGE FRIEND
V QPR

35

GUESS THE CLUB

Can you work out which European Club each set of clues is pointing to?

1 ANSWER

2 ANSWER

3 ANSWER

4 ANSWER

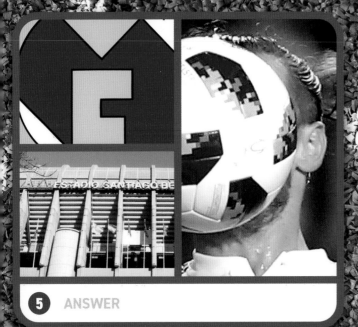

5 ANSWER

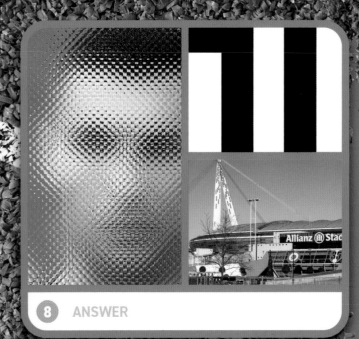

8 ANSWER

6 ANSWER

9 ANSWER

7 ANSWER

10 ANSWER

ANSWERS ON PAGE 62

Magic MOMENT

FAREWELL *Ayresome Park*

FIXTURE: First Division

DATE: Sunday, 30 April 1995

SCORE: Middlesbrough 2 Luton Town 1

VENUE: Ayresome Park

ATTENDANCE: 23,903

John Hendrie wrote his name into Middlesbrough folklore by scoring the final competitive goal at Ayresome Park in April 1995. On an emotional afternoon, as fans bade farewell to the old ground, there was also an important fixture to play for Bryan Robson's promotion-chasing team.

After recovering from a calf injury, the Boro player-manager named himself in the starting line-up for this final home game against Luton Town but this was to be Hendrie's day.

The tiny Scot opened the scoring on the stroke of half-time and after Luton equalised on 63 minutes, he restored Boro's lead nine minutes later with his second goal of the game.

The win as good as secured promotion as it took Boro to within one point of certain promotion to the Premiership.

5

RYAN
SHOTTON

Can you identify the five Boro stars?...

MIDDLESBROUGH FOOTBALL CLUB 1876

1

2

3

4

5

40

ANSWERS ON PAGE 62

...and the three here?

⑥ ⑦ ⑧

WHO ARE YER?

10

MARTIN
BRAITHWAITE

#BOY'SGOTSKILLS

THE FLIP FLAP

Practise! Practise! Practise!

1. Start by getting familiar with the leg movement.

Push the ball with the outside of your foot.

TIP: Try performing the movement while hopping

TIP: Practise performing the movement while moving forwards and backwards

2. Then move your foot around the ball and bring it back in towards your body.

AKA 'the Elastico'
This move is used by many players and was made famous first by Rivelino in the 1970s and more recently by Ronaldinho. It is a simple technique and done right, really works! The idea behind it is to unbalance your defender by moving the ball one way before using some tricky footwork to move off in another direction!

3. Once you're familiar with the movement, try it while dribbling the ball forward.

TIP: Work on perfecting the technique, then when you're ready you can start moving the ball further away from your body to really confuse your defender

4. Push the ball with the outside of your foot, away from your body. As your defender moves in the direction of the ball...

5. ...Move your foot around the ball, drag it back across your body and move off in the other direction.

We take a look at three great Boro games from last season...

«REWIND

QPR 0 BORO 3
SATURDAY 20 JANUARY 2018

A comprehensive performance - including a blockbuster from George Friend, and Adama Traore's first ever Boro goal - saw the Teessiders deservedly take all three points and record the biggest away win of the weekend in the Football League.

Daniel Ayala headed them into a 25th minute lead after Ben Gibson flicked on from a Grant Leadbitter corner. Our next goal came from a most unexpected source, but was arguably worth the 62-game wait since his previous goal as George Friend, 25 yards out, took aim and rifled in a left-footed shot.

We went three up on 85 as Adama Traore linked up with Rudy Gestede and raced away from defenders to drill in a low shot.

BORO 3 LEEDS UNITED 0
FRIDAY 2 MARCH 2018

Conditions weren't great, it was cold with a swirling wind and occasional flurries of snow, but the first career hat-trick from Patrick Bamford, now ironically with Leeds, eased Boro to a comfortable win.

The breakthrough came with just over half an hour played when Downing swept over a cross from the right and Bamford tucked in very neatly from around ten yards.

Then, six minutes later, Adama Traore burst through the middle in the Leeds half and played a low pass out wide to Bamford who took control, set himself and drilled low to score his second.

Prior to this game, the previous Boro player to score a hat-trick at the Riverside was Afonso Alves in an 8-1 win over Manchester City in 2008.

Bamford re-wrote that record with 67 minutes played when Pontus Jansson blocked a shot from Traore, the ball ran loose and he clinically drilled it low past Felix Wiedwald.

DERBY COUNTY 1 BORO 2
SATURDAY 21 APRIL 2018

This was one of the best 90-minute performances under Tony Pulis in the second half of the season - some say the best.

Mo Besic cut past one challenge inside the box before cracking in a shot that was too powerful for Scott Carson for his first goal in Boro colours.

Jonny Howson clipped the bar with a 20-yard shot before Britt Assombalonga was given the freedom of the penalty area and time to pick his spot - he needed no second invitation.

In the second minute of injury-time Derby's David Nugent scored a penalty, but this was a win that was thoroughly merited.

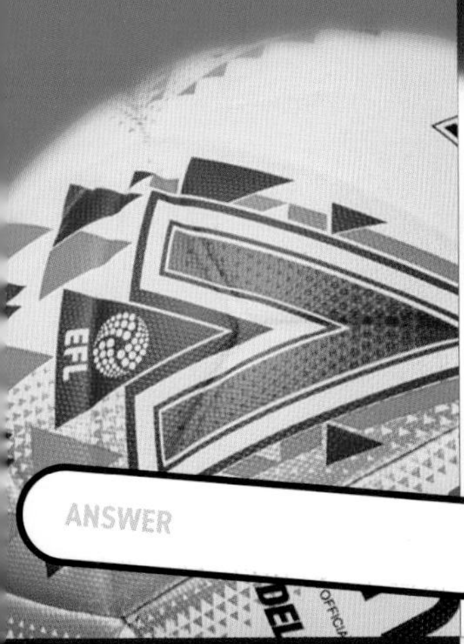

1 Who scored Middlesbrough's first League goal last season?

ANSWER

2 What was the score when Boro knocked Aston Villa out of the League Cup?

ANSWER

3 Who top scored last season with 15 goals across all competitions?

ANSWER

4 How many points did Middlesbrough finish the 2017/18 season with?

ANSWER

5 How many clean sheets did Boro keep in the League in 2017/18?

ANSWER

6 Which player made the most League appearances in 2017/18 with 46?

ANSWER

2017/18 END OF TERM EXAM

How much did you learn about Boro's last campaign?

7 Who was Boro's first win of the 2017/18 season against?

ANSWER

8 Which three Boro players all received ten yellow cards in the League last season?

ANSWER

9 Who scored the goals when Boro beat Birmingham City 2-0 at the Riverside?

ANSWER

10 How many goals did Middlesbrough score in the League last season?

ANSWER

ANSWERS ON PAGE 62

We take a look at three important matches coming up for Boro in the second half of the season...

West Brom at The Hawthorns
Saturday 2 February 2019

West Brom did well to hold on to most of their players in the summer, meaning they started the season with one of the strongest squads in the Championship and they'll end it that way too.

Not just that, but former Boro Academy coach Graeme Jones joined as assistant-manager to the hugely-respected Darren Moore not long after playing his part in Belgium's third place finish in the World Cup.

The aim for the Baggies this season is to reach 100 points and an immediate return to the Premier League.

But it is another return that will interest many, that of Tony Pulis to the Hawthorns as he aims to derail the promotion push of his former side.

Brentford at The Riverside
Saturday 9 March 2019

Many Boro fans may point to the home game with Leeds a month earlier as being bigger than this one, and it may turn out that way.

But Brentford were one of the most improved and consistent sides under Dean Smith last season and if that improvement is continued in the second half of this campaign, then The Bees will be right up there among the promotion contenders.

Brentford haven't won in Middlesbrough since 1938! But they ran us mighty close last year. Their Griffin Park home has always been a difficult place for opposition teams and if they get their act together away from home they might just be serious players.

With ten games to go after this one, the countdown to the end of the season is well and truly on!

Stoke City at The Riverside
Friday 19 April 2019

Who knows what will be at stake when these two meet on Good Friday? It's the second last home game of the season for us and the first of two games in four days as we are due to visit Aitor Karanka's Nottingham Forest on Easter Monday.

It was the opening game of the Premier League season when we last played Stoke at the Riverside and with just three games remaining after this one, there's every chance there will all to play for this time with no room for any mistakes.

A big crowd is expected for what could be a very big game!

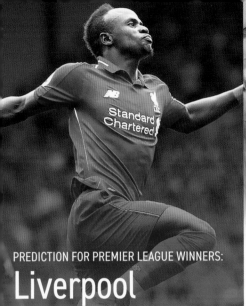

PREDICTION FOR PREMIER LEAGUE WINNERS:

Liverpool

YOUR PREDICTION:

PREDICTION FOR CHAMPIONSHIP WINNERS:

Middlesbrough

YOUR PREDICTION:

PREDICTION FOR FA CUP WINNERS:

Brighton & Hove Albion

YOUR PREDICTION:

PREDICTION FOR PREMIER LEAGUE RUNNERS-UP:

Manchester City

YOUR PREDICTION:

PREDICTION FOR CHAMPIONSHIP RUNNERS-UP:

Derby County

YOUR PREDICTION:

2018/19 PREDICTIONS

Here are our predictions for the 2018/19 season.

What do you think will happen?

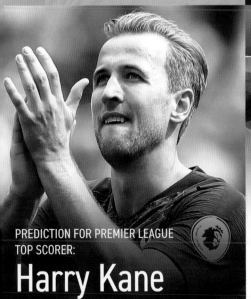

PREDICTION FOR PREMIER LEAGUE TOP SCORER:

Harry Kane

YOUR PREDICTION:

PREDICTION FOR CHAMPIONSHIP TOP SCORER:

Britt Assombalonga

YOUR PREDICTION:

PREDICTION FOR LEAGUE CUP WINNERS:

Burnley

YOUR PREDICTION:

47

#BOY'S GOT SKILLS
THE OKOCHA STEP OVER

Jay-Jay Okocha was one of the best tricksters the Premier League has ever seen. He was effortless in getting past his opponents and here we take a look at how to perform one of his most famous moves...

1. While running...

...roll the ball with the inside of your right foot across your body to the left.

2. Fake like you're going to hit it with your left foot...

TIP:
Roll the ball far enough out across your body so it doesn't get stuck under your feet.

Tip:
Practise until you can master the move off both feet!

3. ...but step over it instead!

4. While you're performing the step over...

...do a quick body feint to the right to help throw off your opponent.

5. Continue going left...

...leaving your opponent wondering what just happened!

8

ADAM
CLAYTON

49

GREAT GAFFERS

Boro have been blessed with a host of great managers down the years - here we take a brief look at four of our finest.

BRUCE RIOCH

Having been appointed Middlesbrough manager in February 1986, Bruce Rioch enjoyed a memorable first full season in charge as he guided Boro to the runners-up spot in the Third Division in 1986/87. That promotion to the Second Division was memorably achieved against a backdrop of serious financial problems at the club at the time.

The famous centre-back pairing of Tony Mowbray and Gary Pallister really came to the fore under Rioch's reign as boss, and the team secured back-to-back promotions in 1987/88. Boro's elevation to the top flight came following an exciting and eventful play-off campaign, as Rioch's men overcame Bradford City in the semi-finals, before securing promotion with a two-legged victory over Chelsea in the final.

Rioch managed the club in the First Division the following season and later in his successful managerial career took in spells with Millwall, Bolton Wanderers, Arsenal and Norwich City.

BRYAN ROBSON

After a glittering trophy-laden career with Manchester United, former England captain Bryan Robson became player/manager at Middlesbrough in 1994. Securing the services of such a high profile individual was a great coup for Boro, and Robson did not disappoint – leading the club to the Premier League and three Wembley finals during his six-year spell as boss.

Robson's time at the helm coincided with the club's move from Ayresome Park to The Riverside. In his first season in management, Robson ensured that the club said farewell to the old ground in the best possible way as they were crowned Division One champions and headed off to begin life at the Riverside as a Premier League club.

Despite relegation in 1996/97, Robson led Boro back to the Premier League at the first attempt. As well as attracting superstar players such as Juninho and Fabrizio Ravanelli to the club, Robson also led Boro to three major cup final appearances during his time as manager.

STEVE McCLAREN

After taking over at The Riverside in 2001, Steve McClaren guided Middlesbrough to the most successful spell in the club's history.

McClaren had gained an excellent reputation as one of the finest coaches in the game and had helped Manchester United to their amazing treble success in his first season assisting Sir Alex Ferguson at Old Trafford.

He led Boro to the FA Cup semi-final in his first season at the club and a twelfth placed finish in the Premier League. The 2003/04 season saw Boro lift the League Cup as the club won its first major honour after McClaren's men defeated Bolton Wanderers 2-1 at the Millennium Stadium in Cardiff.

The League Cup success also resulted in the club qualifying for competitive European football for the first time. In McClaren's final season at the club they enjoyed a historic and thrilling adventure in the UEFA Cup where they eventually faced Sevilla in the final. Such was McClaren's success at Boro, his next role was as manager of the England national team.

AITOR KARANKA

Former Real Madrid defender Aitor Karanka led Middlesbrough to the 2015 Play-Off final at Wembley and then on to Premier League promotion the following season.

After a successful playing career in his homeland, Spaniard Karanka was appointed assistant manager at Real Madrid by newly-appointed boss Jose Mourinho in June 2010. After three years at the Bernabeu, Karanka went in search of a position as manager and took the reins at Middlesbrough in November 2013.

In his first full season at the helm, Karanka saw his side mount a serious bid for automatic promotion, but they ended the season fourth and in the end-of-season play-offs. After defeating Brentford in the semi-finals, Boro missed out on promotion as they suffered a disappointing 2-0 defeat to Norwich City in the Wembley final. However, Karanka rallied the troops and the following season the club won automatic promotion to the Premier League as they ended the 2015/16 campaign as runners-up to champions Burnley.

FIRST ELEVEN

Choose your all-time First Eleven, put their names and numbers on the back of the shirts, then colour them in!

SPOT THE BALL

The ball is missing from this photo, where should it be?

WHAT BALL?

Can you figure out which is the real ball in this photo?

A B C D E F G H

19

STEWART
DOWNING

Boro secured the services of Dutch striker Jimmy Floyd Hasselbaink in the summer of 2004 following his release from Chelsea. Forming a great strike partnership with Australian international Mark Viduka, Hasselbaink's goals helped the club record their highest top-flight finish in 2004/05.

He made an instant impact at the Riverside as he netted a last-gasp equaliser on the opening day of the season to secure a 2-2 with Newcastle United. He bagged a memorable hat-trick in a 4-0 romp away to Blackburn Rovers in October and ended the season as leading scorer with 16 goals, 13 of which came in the Premier League.

The 2006 UEFA Cup Final in Eindhoven proved to be Hasselbaink's final game for the club after scoring 34 goals in 89 games.

BORN:

27 MARCH 1972 · PARAMARIBO, SURINAME

POSITION:

STRIKER

BORO DEBUT:

MIDDLESBROUGH 2–2 NEWCASTLE UNITED
PREMIERSHIP (GOAL ON DEBUT) · 14 AUGUST 2004

ALL CLUBS:

TELSTAR, AZ, CAMPOMAIORENSE, BOAVISTA, LEEDS UNITED, ATLETICO MADRID, CHELSEA, MIDDLESBROUGH, CHARLTON ATHLETIC, CARDIFF CITY

BORO APPEARANCES:

APPEARANCES	LEAGUE	FA CUP	LEAGUE CUP	OTHERS
89	58	8	3	20

BORO GOALS:

GOALS	LEAGUE	FA CUP	LEAGUE CUP	OTHERS
34	23	3	1	7

STAT ATTACK
JIMMY FLOYD HASSELBAINK

HOLLAND INTERNATIONAL:

APPEARANCES	GOALS
23	9

INTERNATIONAL DEBUT:

27 MAY 1988 · HOLLAND 0–0 CAMEROON

HERO HUNT

Here is a list of 20 Boro heroes. All but one of their surnames are hidden in the grid, can you work out who is missing?

```
A V E A T S U B F L S B L R G S P K J O S W
C A B E I L L E N A V A R S H R O T T H B J
D M N R A T Y A J R M H I K S L A P R K I P
B T A D J P I E V A J U Z G N R B E I J Y D
M H N V W B E P I E T Z N E R D D A M J O M
E W C G T M Y O V R N I X Q N U Q R T E V D
A K F P F O Q U Z H O F N C A D A S X I B E
J N U K S W D C I O I G E G K B E O A C W P
A N C X W B B O A T E N G F Q P I N L S Q M
H Z E R G R I S H M J M R U I N B H Z N U G
K I Z O Q A L M N S S O U T H G A T E M E O
I T L N K Y J E R K G E F B C L U A O Y U K
Y O W U G X F A U Y E R L C B P I D V J D A
T H D Y L W I J V S I S O L D C H E L E R D
A I X U C O A H T R D E V O I A F F L Z U N
V C D A F T H X U B N E W U C T S R B R E M
M K H P G V K N Q E T N K G F G X E J U H F
H T E B A J W T I U I M B H A J D T P C O W
Y O D I M T S U R N Z A Y P A B M A D K I E
U N B Q T S O L G V U S E M V R C E L N X T
I R M G E F F D C Z D J O Q M S D H N W R O
N O I N A L E X C W R Y P F S O Q W U P T G
S Z U S R K R H N G O N E U M A N N I O N O
J O B C E V G Y S X B L I L A W D Z E C N I
S C K M H P Q P U Q N T N W K M S C X R K F
```

George **Boateng**	John **Hickton**	Nigel **Pearson**	Graeme **Souness**
George **Camsell**	**Juninho**	Franck **Queudrue**	Gareth **Southgate**
Brian **Clough**	Willie **Maddren**	Fabrizio **Ravanelli**	Mark **Viduka**
Stewart **Downing**	Wilf **Mannion**	Mark **Schwarzer**	David **Wheater**
George **Hardwick**	Tony **Mowbray**	Bernie **Slaven**	Bolo **Zenden**

ANSWERS ON PAGE 62

SHIRT SHUFFLE

1 RLVOELPOI

2 ALUMHF

3 FEEHFLDIS NIEUDT

4 RNGBIHMMIA TIYC

5 TEWS AMH DUTNIE

6 YCTSLRA LAPEAC

Here are the away shirts of twelve football clubs, but their team names have been jumbled up!

Can you figure out who's who?

7 OONEUMTBRUH

8 NQESEU RKAP GRARNES

9 KOETS TCIY

10 WESATNELC TUNEDI

11 ROTPENS HRTNO NDE

12 NATOS LAVIL

Magic MOMENT

LEAGUE CUP *Glory*

FIXTURE:	League Cup Final
DATE:	Sunday, 29 February 2004
SCORE:	Middlesbrough 2 Bolton Wanderers 1
VENUE:	Millennium Stadium, Cardiff
ATTENDANCE:	72, 634

Boudewijn Zenden capped off a Man of the Match performance with Boro's all-important second goal in the 2004 League Cup Final.

Boro had made a dream start to the final against Bolton Wanderers when Joseph-Desire Job met a second minute cross from Zenden to open the scoring at Cardiff's Millennium Stadium.

Five minutes later and Zenden went from provider to scorer as he converted a penalty to put Boro firmly in the driving seat at 2-0.

Bolton pulled a goal back through Kevin Davies after 21 minutes but Steve McClaren's side hung on for victory to secure the club's first major honour.

4

32Red

DANIEL
AYALA

How's your knowledge of the laws of the game?

You think you can do better than the man in the middle?
Here's your chance to prove it...

HEY REF!

1. Martin Braithwaite shoots for goal from 25 yards. His fierce drive deflects off your head, wrong-footing the keeper, on its way into the back of the net. What's your call?

A: You award an indirect free-kick to the opposition.
B: It's a goal!
C: You give a drop-ball from where you were hit with ball.

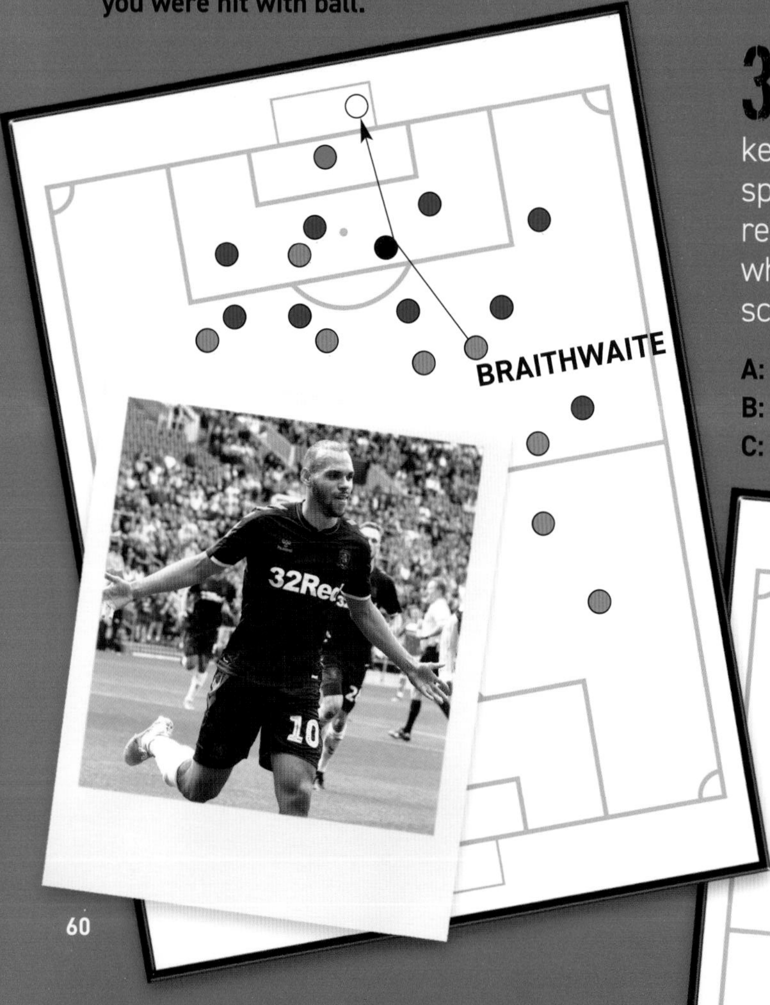

2. Britt Assombalonga strikes for goal from six yards, but as he shoots, the ball bursts and stops just before the goal line. Alert, he follows up and taps the ball home. What's your call?

A: It's a goal!
B: You award a penalty kick to Boro.
C: No goal and you restart with a drop ball where the ball burst.

3. Martin Braithwaite sends the keeper the wrong way from the penalty spot, but his effort hits the post and rebounds straight to Britt Assombalonga who rifles the ball into the net to score. What is your decision?

A: It's a goal!
B: The spot kick has to be retaken.
C: You award an indirect free-kick to the opposition.

BRAITHWAITE

BRAITHWAITE · ASSOMBALONGA

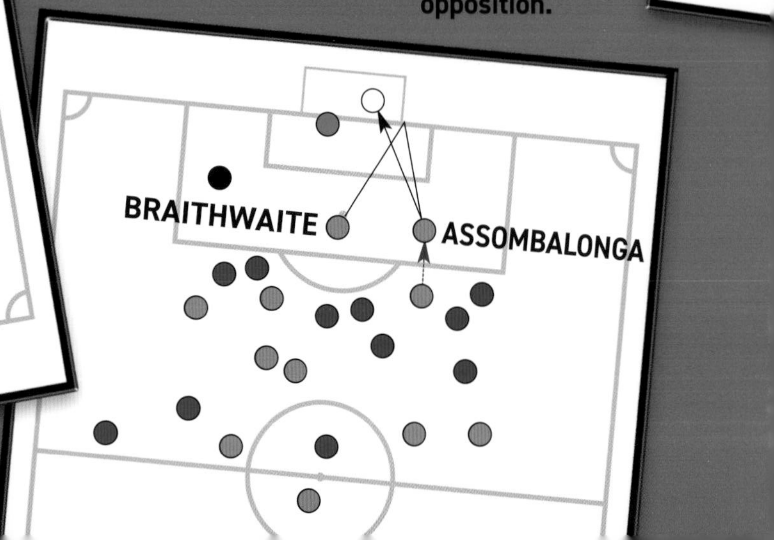

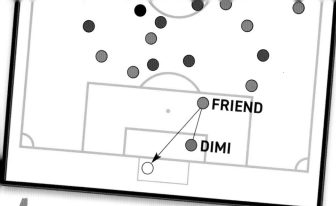

4. Dimi attempts to take a quick goal kick, but to his horror, it hits George Friend who is still in the penalty area and the ball deflects into his own net. What's your call, ref?

A: It's a goal!

B: A corner kick to the opposing team

C: The goal kick has to be retaken.

5. Standing in his own penalty area, Dimi catches the ball directly from teammate George Friend's throw-in. What is your decision?

A: Everything's fine. Play on.

B: You award the opposing team an indirect free-kick.

C: A yellow card for Dimi and a penalty for the opposing team.

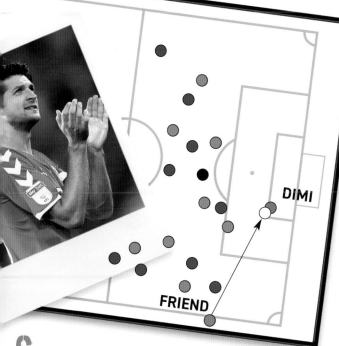

6. You have decided Martin Braithwaite's spot kick must be re-taken after an infringement by the keeper. This time Britt Assombalonga steps forward to take the kick. Is that allowed?

A: No, I award an indirect free kick to the opposition.

B: Yes, any Boro player can re-take the penalty.

C: No, the player who took the initial spot kick, Martin Braithwaite, must retake the kick.

7. You have awarded a drop ball. As you drop the ball, George Friend and the opposing player both kick the ball at exactly the same time before it hits the turf. What's your ruling?

A: You show a yellow card to both players for ungentlemanly conduct.

B: You drop the ball again.

C: Play on.

8. Britt Assombalonga is on the scoresheet again, tapping in from only three yards out. When he scores, he is slightly ahead of the last defender, but in line with the goalkeeper. What is your decision?

A: Goal. In line with the keeper is not offside.

B: Goal disallowed. Assombalonga is offside. To be onside, he must be in line with the second last opponent or the ball.

C: Goal. A player can't be offside inside the six-yard box.

9. Britt Assombalonga takes a long throw in aiming for the head of Ryan Shotton. No-one makes contact with the ball and it bounces into the net direct from Assombalonga's throw. What's your call, ref?

A: Goal. Providing there was an attempt to play the ball.

B: Goal. As long as the throw-in was taken correctly.

C: No Goal. A goal can never be scored direct from a throw in.

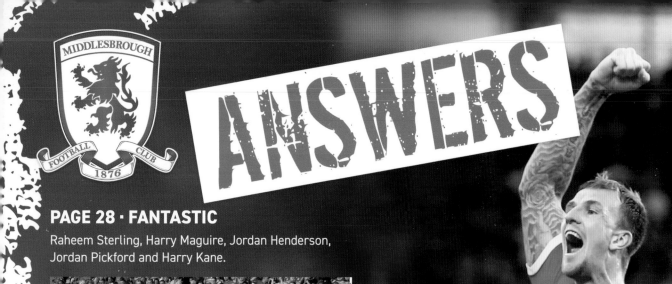

ANSWERS

PAGE 28 · FANTASTIC

Raheem Sterling, Harry Maguire, Jordan Henderson, Jordan Pickford and Harry Kane.

PAGE 36 · GUESS THE CLUB

1. Ajax. 2. Paris Saint-Germain. 3. Bayern Munich.
4. Sporting Lisbon. 5. Real Madrid. 6. Arsenal. 7. Celtic.
8. Juventus. 9. Barcelona. 10. Club Brugge.

PAGE 40 · WHO ARE YER?

1. Britt Assombalonga. 2. Darren Randolph.
3. George Friend. 4. Jonny Howson. 5. Aden Flint.
6. Martin Braithwaite. 7. Lewis Wing. 8. Adam Clayton

PAGE 45 · 2017/18 END OF TERM EXAM

1. Rudy Gestede. 2. Aston Villa 0 Middlesbrough 2.
3. Britt Assombalonga. 4. 76. 5. 16. 6. Darren Randolph.
7. Sheffield United. 8. Adam Clayton, George Friend and
Grant Leadbitter. 9. Britt Assombalonga scored both goals.
10. 67.

PAGE 53 · SPOT THE BALL

PAGE 53
WHAT BALL?

Ball C.

PAGE 56 · HERO HUNT

Mark Schwarzer.

PAGE 57 · SHIRT SHUFFLE

1. Liverpool. 2. Fulham. 3. Sheffield United.
4. Birmingham City. 5. West Ham United.
6. Crystal Palace. 7. Bournemouth.
8. Queens Park Rangers. 9. Stoke City.
10. Newcastle United. 11. Preston North End.
12. Aston Villa.

PAGE 60 · HEY REF!

1. B. 2. C. 3. A. 4. C. 5. B. 6. B. 7. B. 8. B. 9. C.